49 Ways to Steal the Cookie Jar

Copyright © 2013, 2022 by James Warwood

Published by Curious Squirrel Press

All rights reserved

No part of this book may be used, stored or reproduced in any manner whatsoever without written permission from the author or publisher.

Book cover design by: James Warwood
Book interior design by: Mala Letra / Lic. Sara F. Salomon

ISBN: 9798420960820
ebook ISBN: B00GYSLE20

THE EXCUSE ENCYCLOPEDIA

Book Two: 49 Ways to Steal the Cookie Jar

James Warwood

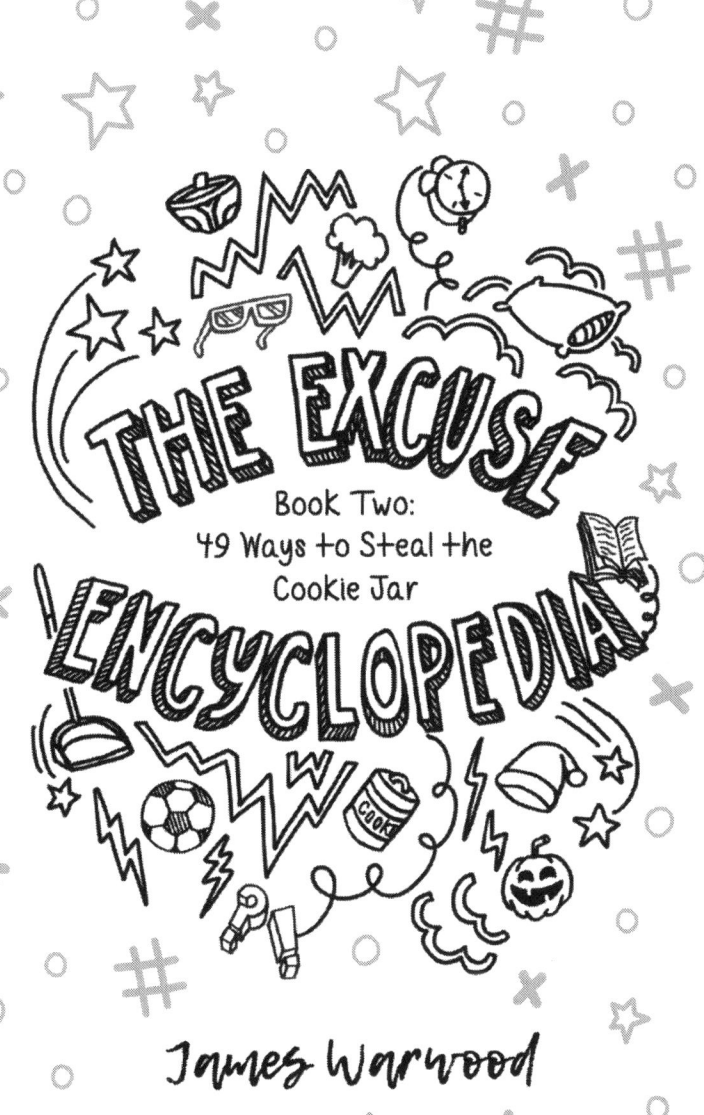

BOOK TWO

Ways to Steal the Cookie Jar

James Warwood

1. BUY A TRAMPOLINE

I'm practising my Trampoline routine for the next Olympic Games . . .

. . . I know the kitchen isn't the best place to practise, but I honestly just picked this room at random.

2. STAND IN FERTILIZER

My science teacher taught me that plants grow faster in the sunshine, when they're well watered, and planted in fertilizer rich with nutrients . . .

. . . so this should speed up my growth spurt!

3. CREATE THE MIRACLE COOKIE

After endless nights of research, I've discovered a cookie combination that produces a truly miraculous result . . .

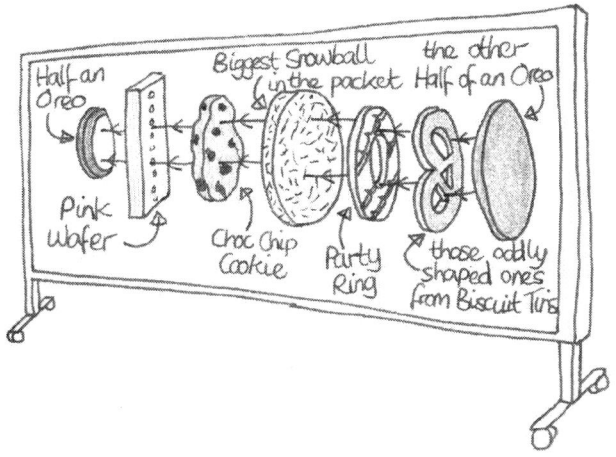

. . . one bite and you'll never be hungry again. As you can see, I've now finished the 'Theory Stage', so I'm going to need the Cookie Jar so I can begin the 'Testing Stage'.

4. BIRD OF PREY

This is Robby, my pet budgie . . .

. . . he can smell a cookie from a mile away and his razor sharp claws can rip through metal. No matter where you hide the Cookie Jar, Robbie will find it, he will ferociously attack it, and I will have a cookie before bedtime!

5. THE COOKIE MAINTENANCE MAN

We received a call from a Mr. Rogers about a serious problem with his Cookie Jar...

... I'll happily take a look at it now. By the way, the callout charge is 2 Chocolate Bourbons, and the repair charges can range from a Jam Doughnut to a Double Fudge Chocolate Cake.

6. THE THREE CUP TRICK

The cookie is under one of these three cups. Pick the right one and you'll win the cookie . . .

. . . Wow! I must have made the cookie disappear by magic! Did I mention it costs a cookie for every guess, which means you now owe me three cookies.

7. HAND-DRAWN COOKIE WATCH

My new hand-drawn watch says it's Cookie o'clock in 3 minutes . . .

. . . and again in 18 minutes, in 33 minutes, in 48 minutes, and in 63 minutes too. So I'm going to need the Cookie Jar to keep up with my new watch!

8. An Important Question

Can cookies bring you lasting happiness? . . .

. . . give me the Cookie Jar and I will give you a comprehensive written answer in 2-3 hours.

James Warwood

9. TRAIN A CHIMP

This is my trainee Chimp, Boris . . .

. . . I'm training him to sneak into the kitchen, climb up the wall and steal the Cookie Jar. It's early days, but I think I'm making good progress.

49 Ways to Steal the Cookie Jar

10. ASSEMBLE AN ELITE COOKIE SQUAD

Say hello to my Elite Squad of Deadly Cookie Snatchers...

...Cookie Squad, get me that Cookie Jar.

James Warwood

11. BUILD A PET PYRAMID

12. FAKE DOCTOR'S PHONE CALL

"Hello this is Katie . . ." *pause* "Good Afternoon Doctor, do you have the results from my tests . . .

. . . really, I have a Cookie-Deficiency. . ." *pause* "If I don't eat enough cookies I'll transform into a little monster and become a danger to society . . ." *pause* "And the treatment is to eat cookies until you can discover a cure . . ." *pause* "Okay, I'll pass on the information to my parents and thank you Doctor."

13. CHARITY APPEAL

Our school is raising money for charity. All my friends are doing the normal stuff -- sponsored fun runs, sponsored bike rides, sponsored silence. So I've decided to do something completely different . . .

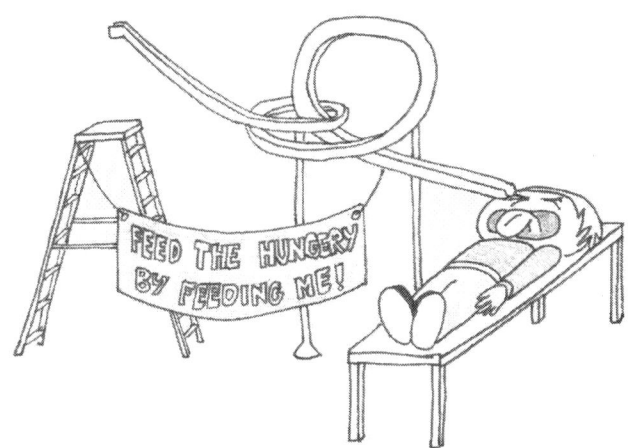

. . . I'm going to do a sponsored Cookie-a-thon. My target is to raise $10,000 by eating 10,000 cookies. Would you like to be the first person to sponsor me?

14. BEWARE THE CROCOSECT!

Oh no! A plague of Crocosects are coming down our street. What? You've never heard of a Crocosect? . . .

. . . they've got the head of a Crocodile, the body of an insect, and the appetite of a teenage boy! Pass me the Cookie Jar and I'll hide it under my pillow, then you grab the fruit bowl and hide it under my little brother's pillow.

15. GROW YOUR FINGERNAILS

What's that Mum? Why am I growing my finger nails? . . .

. . . no particular reason. Haven't you got some ironing to do?

16. THE PIPE PIPER

I bought this tin whistle and it seems to work wonders on the rats...

...if only they liked Custard Creams more than Mini Cheddars!

17. WRITE A LETTER

I know how to unite the world in peace and love . . .

. . . all we need to do is share our cookies. For the best results I suggest Jammie Dodgers.

18. WINGARDIUM LEVIOSA

For my home-made wand I've used hair from the tail of the neighbour's dog as the core and a 7 and ½ inch twig from the garden...

... Hermione makes the Levitation Charm look much easier in the films!

19. MONSTER ATTACK

Mum, mum, the Cookie Monster smashed through the TV screen . . .

. . . quick, hand me the Cookie Jar and I'll run to my room, jam a chair under the handle, and keep our Cookie Jar safe from that blue, fuzzy monster.

20. THE HOLY RECIPE

I've spent the last few months studying at the Sacred Monastery on the peak of Crumble Mountain...

...I have studied the Ancient Scrolls passed down by 'The Ancestors' from generation to generation. They contain the holy recipe for the perfect batch of cookies. According to my translation, they may only be prepared and baked by a loving mother and eaten by her most worthy son.

James Warwood

21. LEARN MARTIAL ARTS

Be warned, I've mastered Karate..

... I can karate chop through eight Bourbons, karate kick through fourteen Chocolate Fingers and face slam through a Jammy Wagon Wheelie. So don't mess with me! Now hand over the Cookie Jar and no harm shall come to your or your cookies.

49 Ways to Steal the Cookie Jar

22. USE ANCIENT WAR TACTICS

I tried using ancient war tactics I learned in last week's History lesson . . .

. . . but I'm guessing the Trojans didn't conquer a kingdom on an empty stomach.

23. CHAMELEON MAN

The chameleon has solved the 'Cookie Jar' problem with the combination of camouflague, suction pads, and a sticky extendable tongue . . .

. . . should have tried the camouflage. Darn slippy kitchen tiles!

24. CREATE AN AMAZING INVENTION

I think I've cracked the world's energy crisis with my amazing invention -- The Crumble-nator...

... it runs on cookie crumbs by sweeping them up and churns them into pure energy. It's only in the experimental phase, so for the good of all humanity and the environment I'm going to need the Cookie Jar.

James Warwood

25. TRY A GIANT ELECTRO-MAGNET

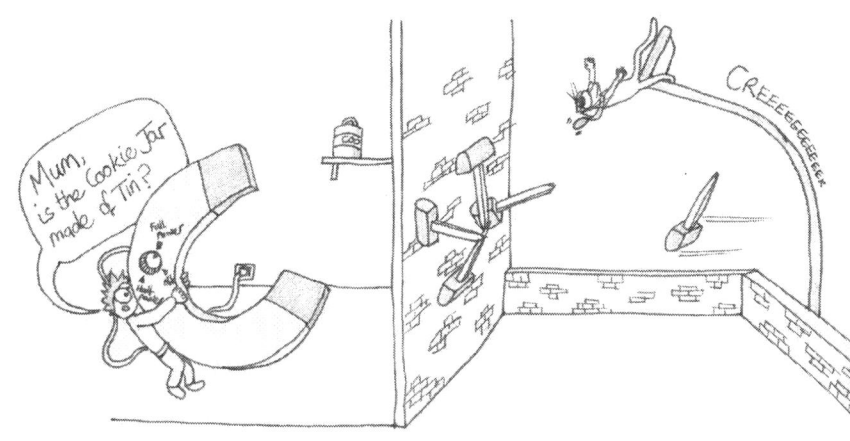

26. VISIT FROM THE COOKIE INSPECTOR

Good morning Sir. I'm with the Government's Special Branch for the National Cookie Inspection. My colleagues will be here shortly to do the measure, sniff, weight, and crumble tests. I'm here to do the 'Taste Test' . . .

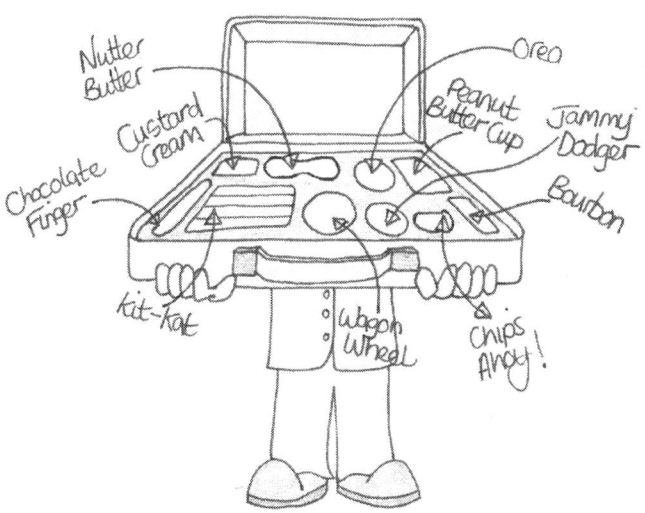

. . . I'm going to need a sample of every type of Cookie in your house. Then I'll take them back to our Government Labs for testing and send your results in the post. By the way, the 'Poor Cookie Quality Fine' is $1,000. Good luck!

27. DO ALIENS LIKE COOKIES?

For this week's homework I've got to write an essay on one of life's BIG questions. I'm going to tackle a big one -- if aliens exist which cookie would be their favourite? . . .

TRIPLE CHOC
DARK CHOC
MILK CHOC
WHITE CHOC

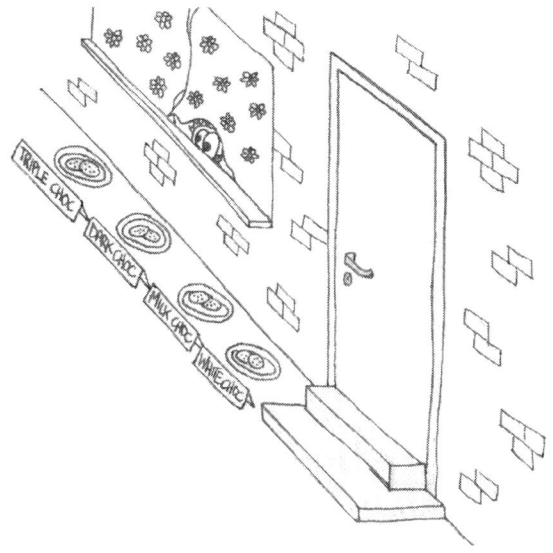

. . . I'm going to leave out different cookies and see which ones are still here in the morning.

49 Ways to Steal the Cookie Jar

28. BORROW YOUR DAD'S FISHING ROD

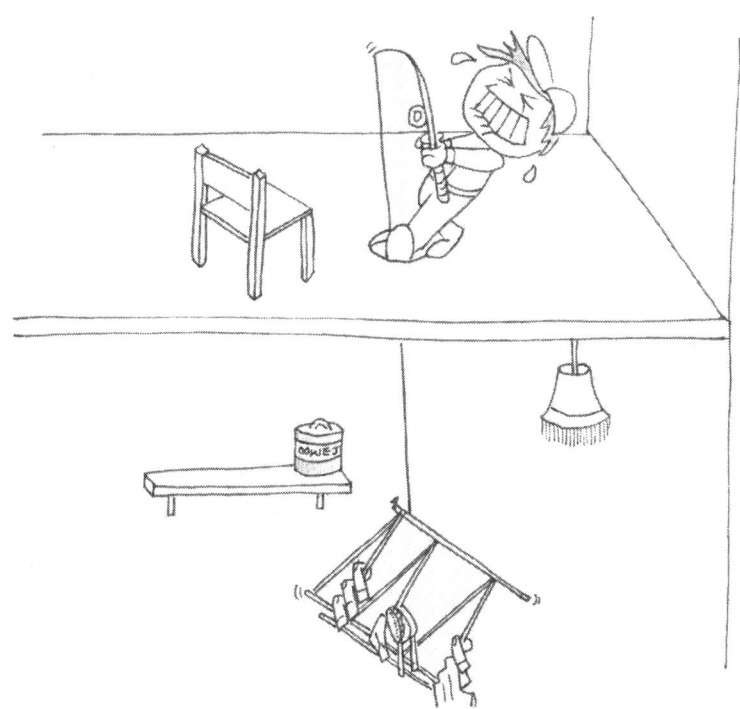

James Warwood

29. RESIZE & REDISTRIBUTE

I've decided that our family Cookie Jar should be split between each member . . .

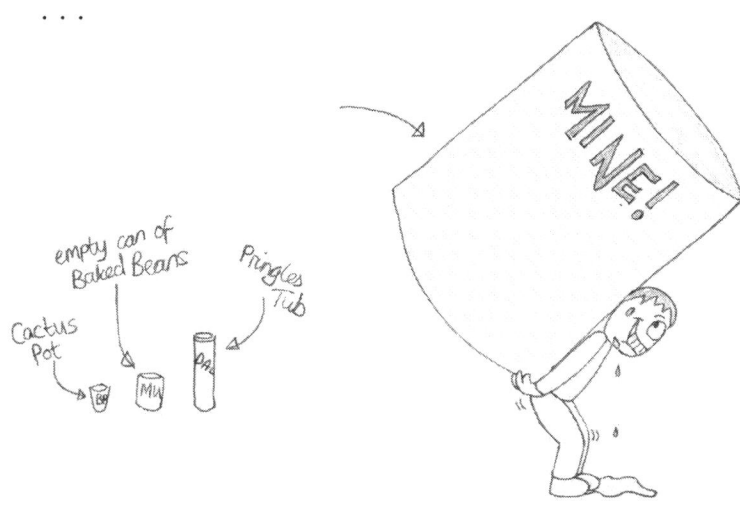

. . . I took many factors into account - average daily consumption, height to weight ratio, and who currently has the highest score on Angry Birds. According to my data analysis, these are our new Cookie Jars. Due to its size I think mine should live in my bedroom.

30. LEARN THE TARZAN SWING

Tarzan would use a Jungle Vine to swing to his target. You won't find any Jungle Vines in the kitchen so I'm using the washing line. and there aren't many solid wood kitchen tables in the Jungle either.

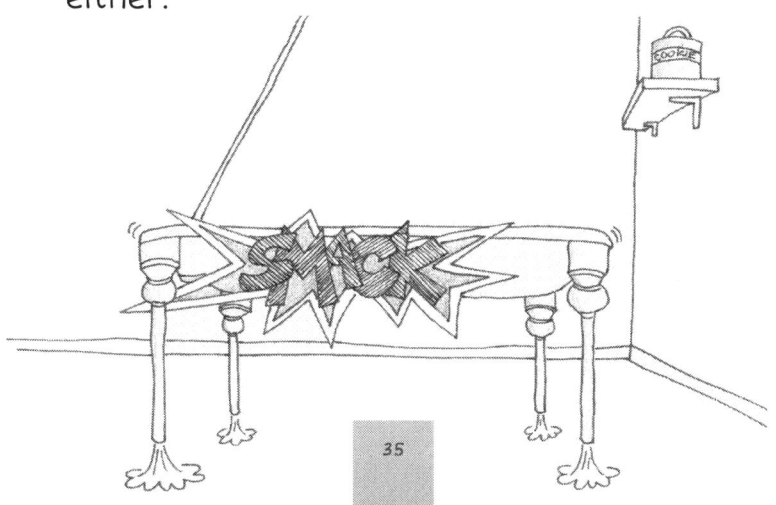

James Warwood

31. BRING IN THE LAWYERS

I didn't want it to come to this but you leave me no choice. This is my team of brilliantly-minded, ruthlessly-cunning Lawyers . . .

. . . they've been building a damning legal case against you -- parental corruption, bribery, blackmail, and organised child slavery. But it'll all go away if you sign over the 'Ownership Contract' of the Cookie Jar to me! It's that simple.

32. NEED SOME GRANDMA BAIT

Dad, I'm going fishing for another Grandma . . .

. . . it's a well-known fact the best bait for Grandma's is shortbread. I'll catch a good one, have a cup of tea and some shortbread with her, and then bring home my prize winning catch. Would you pass me the Cookie Jar, I mean the Bait Box?

33. Home-Made Security Vault

Have you heard the news? Cookie Crime is up by over 500% in our neighbourhood! . . .

. . . but there's no need to panic. I'll happily keep them in my Home-Made Security Vault for safe keeping.

34. THE DECEASED COOKIE JAR

Dad, I have some bad news. While you were out washing the car the Cookie Jar had a massive heart attack and passed away...

... we held a short, touching funeral in the kitchen and then I found the perfect place to bury him.

James Warwood

35. THE 3 RULES OF CHILDHOOD

The three most important rules in childhood: 1) Eat cookies. 2) Give your daughter what she wants all the time. 3) . . .

. . . erm, sorry I've forgotten the last one. Why is my hand still empty?

49 Ways to Steal the Cookie Jar

36. WHAT WOULD ROBIN HOOD DO?

I've decided to adopt the Robin Hood philosophy...

... take from the rich (the Cookie Jar), and give to the poor (my empty stomach).

37. BECOME AN AUTHOR

I've spent the past 6 years of my life researching the nutritional benefits of the Hobnob . . .

. . . my ground-breaking research suggests they have all the nutrients required for everlasting health, happiness, and handsomeness. Here, have a free copy of my bestselling book – 'Hobnobs: The Elixir of Life'.

38. LEARN HYPNOSIS

Look deep into my eyes . . .

. . . empty the contents of the Cookie Jar on my dinner plate. Then cook Spinach & Broccoli Soup for my little brother. And every time he says 'I hate my sister', fill his school lunch box with raw Brussels Sprouts.

39. BECOME THE SHOPPING TROLLEY GHOST!

40. EXTERMINATE THE COOKIES

Our nation is suffering from a terrible infestation - Cookie Termites!! . . .

. . . I know this sounds extreme, but the only way to get rid of them is to eat every single cookie on the planet. Cut off their food supply and we'll kill the vermin! My belly is empty so I'll happily begin the extermination with our Cookie Jar.

James Warwood

41. READ FROM THE BIBLE

Today's reading will be from Genesis 1:42-43 . . .

. . . "And on the 8th day God created cookies, and declared it to be the food of humankind. For the heavenly snack contained everything they needed to live: peace, love, and plenty of chocolate chips." Now let us praise God by opening his sacred Cookie Jar and enjoying his scrumptious creation.

42. INSTALL A COOKIE-METER

Stop right there sir, this is now a 'Parking Meter Zone'...

... you've got to pay using this Cookie Meter: 1 Chocolate Chip Cookie for 1 hour, 1 Double Chocolate Chip Cookie for 2 hours, or 1 Triple Chocolate Chip Cookie for 3 hours or more.

James Warwood

43. BECOME A NUTRITIONIST

I decided that when I grow up I'd like to become a Nutritionist...

... the great thing about being a Nutritionist is you get to decide what you eat. Here's this week's meal list for me and my little brother.

44. THE MOUSE TRAP

DAD!!! COME QUICK!!! THERE'S A MOUSE IN THE COOKIE JAR! . . .

. . . relax Dad, this was just a test of your response time in saving our family's most precious and valued possession. Congratulations, you passed, which means I honour you with the prestigious title 'Protector of the Cookie Jar'. Your next test will measure how much you love your daughter (hint, hint).

45. OFFER TO DO THE DUSTING

I know how busy you are with work, housework, and parenting me. So I've decided I'd give you a helping hand by doing the dusting . . .

. . . I'm starting with the spider's web in the corner above the Cookie Jar.

49 Ways to Steal the Cookie Jar

46. CONSTRUCTION SITE

I'm attempting a world record in Cookie Packaging Construction...

. . . the highest building made entirely out of empty boxes of cookies! I'm so close to the record, all I need is an extra couple of inches. Help me make history by passing me the Cookie Jar.

47. ACQUIRE THE RAW INGREDIENTS

Mum, I need some items for this week's homework: butter, sugar, flour, eggs, chocolate chips, and a bowl...

... I need the butter to make a butter sculpture for my Art homework, sugar to help me count to a thousand for my Maths homework, flour to use as make-up for my Mime performance in Drama, eggs to practise my juggling skills for my Gym homework, chocolate chips for my lunchbox, and a bowl to use as a helmet in our World War II reconstruction in History Class.

48. DISSECTION LESSON

I forgot to tell you last night, we're dissecting a penguin in Science Class tomorrow . . .

. . . don't look so horrified. The chocolate-coated cookie, not the Antarctic-waddling animal. I also forgot to tell you that Mark, Robby, Dean, Chloe, Tanya, George, and Violet are all cookie-tarians* so I said I'd bring them a penguin to dissect from our Cookie Jar.

* Cookie-tarian: someone who refuses to eat any cookie-dough based food due to cruelty to butter.

49. ASK POLITELY

Still no cookie? Why not try asking politely.

. . . go on. If the other 48 ways haven't worked, it's worth a go!

49 Ways to Steal the Cookie Jar

BONUS: RAID THE SHOE RACK

Why am I wearing all the shoes in the house? . . .

. . . No reason!

James Warwood

BONUS: MINECRAFT DAD

If you give me a cookie, I'll create a Minecraft version of you . . .

HAIR

. . . WITH HAIR! (Caution: this will only work if your dad is bald and likes Minecraft).

49 Ways to Steal the Cookie Jar

BONUS: COOKIES CHALLENGE

Have you ever wondered what would happen if someone ate all the cookies in the cookie jar . . .

. . . I have. Want to find out?

James Warwood

BONUS: BORING CONVERSATION

Thanks for the lovely conversation . . .

. . . I do hope you'll find something new to complain about next time while I pretend to listen and eat the entire packet of cookies.

BONUS: CHANGE THE EXPIRATION DATE

It says on the cookie dough packaging that the expiration date is TODAY...

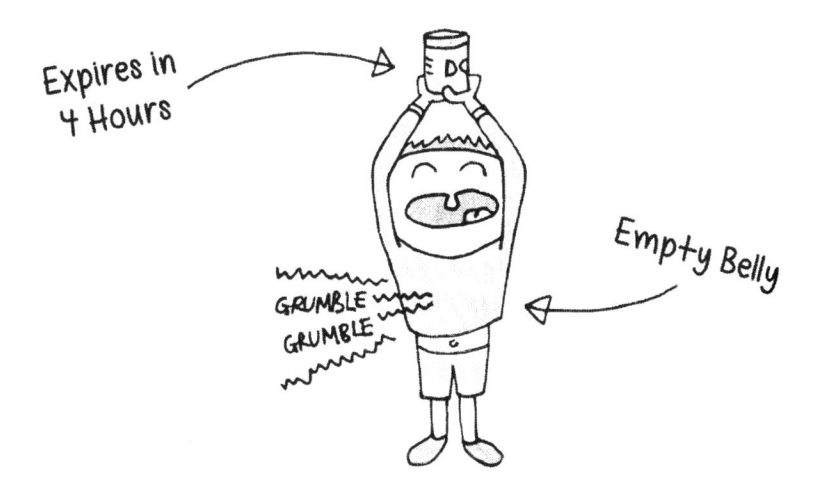

Expires in 4 Hours

Empty Belly

GRUMBLE GRUMBLE

... Quick. Put the oven on and bake it so that it doesn't go to waste. I'll take one for the team and eat them as soon as they cool down.

James Warwood

BONUS: UNRESTRICTED ACCESS

Do you know what would totally help you gain my respect? . . .

UNRESTRICTED ACCESS!

. . . These two magic words in regards to the cookie jar.

BONUS: SHORTBREAD FOR SHORT PEOPLE

After months of tireless campaign I've finally been able to change the law . . .

. . . It is now illegal for tall people to eat shortbread. You tall people can keep your Brandy Snaps and Chocolate Fingers, but hand over all your shortbread or I'll call the police.

James Warwood

BONUS: BANANA TORTURE

Stick em' up . . .

. . . Hand over the cookie jar or the banana gets it!

49 Ways to Steal the Cookie Jar

BONUS: STOCKPILE COOKIE CUTTERS

SURPRISE!!! . . .

. . . I've bought you some brand new cookie cutters. You better hurry up and give them all a go right away.

James Warwood

BONUS: SIX COOKIES

Did you know that you are five times more likely to give me a cookie than win the lottery? . . .

. . . So, give me six cookies and then go buy yourself a lottery ticket.

BONUS: MAKE A CUPPA

I've made you this delicious cuppa tea . . .

. . . So, I'd recommend that you get the cookie jar down immediately and leave it at eye level while you go put your feet up and relax for the next ten to twenty minutes.

James Warwood

BONUS: STRIKE A DEAL

You've got something I want and I've got something you want . . .

. . . I want cookies and you want some peace and quiet. So, sit down and let's start drafting a deal.

ABOUT THE AUTHOR

James Warwood is (usually) very good at writing about himself. So he would like to start by saying that this bio was written on an off day.

He lives on the Welsh Border with his wife, two boys, and carnivorous plant. For some unknown reason he chose a career in Customer Service, mainly because it was indoor work and involves no manual labour. He writes and illustrates children's books by night like a superhero.

Anyway, people don't really read these bios, do they? They want to get on with reading a brand new book or play outside, not wade through paragraphs of text that attempts to make the author sound like a really interesting and accomplished person. Erm . . . drat, I've lost my rhythm.

WHERE TO FIND JAMES ONLINE

Website: www.cjwarwood.com
Goodreads: James Warwood
Instagram: CJWarwood
Twitter: @cjwarwood
Facebook: James Warwood

SO, WHAT'S NEXT?

MIDDLE-GRADE STAND-ALONE FICTION

The Chef Who Cooked Up a Catastrophe
The Boy Who Stole One Million Socks
The Girl Who Vanquished the Dragon

TRUTH OR POOP?

True or false quiz books. Learn something new and laugh as you do it!

Book One: Amazing Animal Facts
Book Two: Spectacular Space Facts
Book Three: Gloriously Gross Facts

THE EXCUSE ENCYCLOPEDIA
Eleven more books to read!

Book 1 - 49 Excuses for Not Tidying Your Bedroom
Book 2 - 49 Ways to Steal the Cookie Jar
Book 3 - 49 Excuses for Not Doing Your Homework
Book 4 - 49 Questions to Annoy Your Parents
Book 5 - 49 Excuses for Skipping Gym Class
Book 6 - 49 Excuses for Staying Up Past Your Bedtime
Book 7 - 49 Excuses for Being Really Late
Book 8 - 49 Excuses For Not Eating Your Vegetables
Book 9 - 49 Excuses for Not Doing Your Chores
Book 10 - 49 Excuses for Getting the Most Out of Christmas
Book 11 - 49 Excuses for Extending Your Summer Holidays
Book 12 - 49 Excuses for Baggin More Candy at Halloween

Or get all 12 titles in 1 MASSIVE book!

The Excuse Encyclopedia: Books 1 - 12

Printed in Great Britain
by Amazon